C000242832

Swan

ENCOUNTERS IN THE WILD

JIM CRUMLEY

Saraband

ONE

I HAVE KEPT the company of swans for more than half my life now. There are doubtless those who will find such devotion disproportionate. They may be right, but as the years pass the swan bond only grows, only strengthens.

I have watched and tried to come close to swans in every corner of the landscapes of my native Scotland from the Solway to Shetland, from Berwickshire to the Uists, and from Buchan Ness to Ardnamurchan. I am as restless a traveller in my own land as a wintering whooper swan. There have also been forays to the north, east and south of England and to Iceland and Alaska. Letters reporting the ways of swans have also reached me from Texas, New Hampshire, Australia and Norway. There have been so many adventures.

But the heart of it all is the story that unfolded – that still unfolds – a few miles from my own doorstep. It concerns a pair of mute swans that live on a loch in Highland Perthshire. In all my travels, I have found nothing like them.

This is not the whole story. Rather it is the beginning of the end of a chapter. The whole story is as old as swans, and it will outlive me by many millennia. But if I might lead you to a certain drystone dyke a hundred feet above the loch on a quiet afternoon of late autumn a few years ago…

◉ ◉ ◉

The birches, the larches, the mountain grasses, the reed bed at the edge of the loch, are all afire, sparkling after sleety rain and in fitful sunlight. It is as if nature has contrived its finest theatrical stage set then gone completely over the top with the colour. The drystone dyke where I sit is so familiar to me I know where the very stones will fit into my back. I have sat here so often, over so many hundreds of hours and for more years than it is good for me to remember. There are stags roaring across the loch, for it is the season of the red deer rut. There are golden eagles in the mountains on both sides of the loch, peregrines and ravens on nearby crags, and otters on the river that thrusts tree-lined banks far out into the loch, making two bays of its northern shore.

But I have come to watch a pair of mute swans. I know of no other mute swans that nest in such a wild situation, nor in such isolation from other swan populations. And surely no swans ever suffered such adversity at the hands of nature itself. For every spring, reliably at the nesting season, the place floods spectacularly. The river, the two bays, a lochan to the north and all the low-lying fields and wetlands are hauled in by the loch. Fences submerge. Trees wade waist-deep. Then the waters fall as quickly as they have risen and the landscape gasps in the dazed aftermath.

The consequences for the swans are fearful. They build a nest in the reed bed. The floods swamp it or wash it away completely. If laying has begun, the eggs are lost. So they build again on the edge of the floodwaters. The waters recede and the new nest is suddenly high and dry and a quarter of a mile from the water's edge. The swans abandon it, often leaving eggs behind, and build again in the reeds. Second floodings are common, in which case the whole process can happen again. Year after year, the birds endure the same ordeal, re-enact the same rituals. They lose nest after nest and clutch after clutch of eggs, and you wonder why on earth they persist.

But they do persist, and have done for twenty years that I know of, and quite possibly for much, much longer. Once, in a single season, I watched them build five nests, lay twenty eggs (and lose fifteen of them), and finally in late July they hatched out a single cygnet. The pen took to the water with it at once, but even then the cob sat for two more weeks – until the fiftieth day – on four infertile eggs. The cygnet was too late and too weak. It never fledged and died within a few weeks, having been abandoned by its parents. Adult swans have no time for weaklings, even a weakling in a brood of one. A fox found it.

Mostly, the swans raise no young. Occasionally they fledge a single cygnet, exceptionally they fledge two. And so they keep the flimsiest of toeholds on their chosen landscape, wild as otters, aloof from all other swans.

I found them in the first place because it is my chosen landscape too. The loch lies at the heart of a territory of mountains, foothills, woods and water-sheets that I think of as the Highland Edge. Lowlands and Highlands collide here and briefly overlap. I cross that threshold of landscapes almost daily in pursuit of nature's secrets. The swans became a part of my landscape. I became a part of theirs.

We communicated. Or, rather, I started to call to them from a particular shore. They learned to associate the call with food. Eventually they would come from as far as half a mile away. Even if I was out of sight when I called. I would emerge from the trees to see them swimming strongly for my shore, thrusting small bow-waves before them. They grunted at me. Sometimes they hissed. I learned the sounds without ever discovering their meaning. But in time they relaxed in my company, and when-ever I called from my shore they sought me out. I was, at the very least, a benevolent presence. My behaviour and the food I brought were reliable.

So when, at the end of one winter, I rowed a raft out into their reed bed and anchored it there, the swans swam alongside, inspecting the work as it proceeded. They swam intrigued around the raft when I went ashore. My theory was that the raft would give them immunity from floods, and therefore the opportunity to nest early, which is crucial for swans.

For example, there is a pair with an island nest on a Lowland farm pond fifty miles from here. They reliably hatch eight eggs in the second week of May, and just as reliably fledge every cygnet. My raft would be the loch pair's "island".

It worked, and it did not work.

It worked because at nesting time they took to the raft at once and it rode out the inevitable floods perfectly. It did not work because a dark conspiracy of natural forces was just beginning.

The pen laid eight eggs in April, an unprecedented event in her story. My cautious optimism soon grew buoyant, but ten days before the eggs were due to hatch they disappeared in the night.

There was a shortlist of obvious culprits: human or fox. Neither was particularly plausible.

Vandalism is all but unheard of on such a shore. Besides, vandals disfigure and destroy; they do not take pains to remove every trace of their energies. But there was no scrap of eggshell left and the nest was quite unmolested. Swan eggs are all but worthless to collectors, and eggs so close to hatching are less than worthless.

A fox would have to make eight uncomfortable swimming journeys, carrying away one egg at a time while the swans stood placidly by. Such things are not in the nature of foxes or swans. I have watched swans turn on foxes and big dogs (a much less predictable threat). This very pair would confidently face up to the Clydesdale horses that are occasionally let loose in the rough fields down the lochside. The cob is the biggest I have ever seen, and a formidable defender of his territory. But *something* slipped through the guard.

For the rest of that spring and summer and autumn, the swans were a partnership of idleness. They drifted around the loch, they fed, they preened, and they swam in to my call. But they did not try to nest again.

◎ ◎ ◎

The birds wintered well. There had been no energy expended on the nesting season. When fourteen whooper swans, Icelandic itinerants, paused on the loch in midwinter, the mute swan cob confronted them fearlessly. He herded them far down the loch and finally charged them so that they all took flight, trumpeting their anxiety.

As a new spring approached, the swans looked unstoppable. The cob was bigger, deeper-chested than ever, and every visible portent was healthy. But the unseen portents were otherwise aligned.

The raft had taken a battering in the February storms. I patched it up and waded it back out into the reed bed, laden with old reeds that I had gathered from the shore. The pen, always the more confiding of the birds, followed almost at my heels. The cob made one unconvinced and unconvincing attempt at nest-building in the reed bed a few yards from the raft. The pen ignored his efforts. When he turned to the raft again, she co-operated enthusiastically. She laid eight eggs in late April, and lost them all in the night after ten days.

Then the swans did an extraordinary thing. In all the years I have watched them they have always built a completely new nest after one particular site had failed. This time, they tidied the raft nest after a two-week rest and the pen climbed on and laid five more eggs. And five more eggs disappeared in the night.

But by this time the conspiracy of natural forces was in full flow, insinuating its presence on two fronts. The first – a marked increase in otter activity on the river – had become more obvious over the winter, and I was slow to recognise its ominous significance for the swans. Otters had always been a part of the river's natural community, but as an uncertain presence, glimpses in dawns and dusks with long absences between glimpses. The river's tendency to swamp the rooty places on the banks where otters love to lie up was a discouragement at certain times of the year. But new artificial holts upstream had helped to consolidate otter life, and more and more I would read their signs on the banks where the river dawdles darkly among alders and hazels towards the loch shore.

Whenever the river receded enough to lay bare a muddy patch at the foot of the banks it would pattern with otter footprints. Tunnels and slides from the top of the bank to the water's edge became more defined. Otter spraints, musky and crammed with fish bones, punctuated the path along the riverbank more and more liberally in small, dark monograms. I began to find half-eaten fish, and once, a newly killed mallard so warm that I climbed into a tree to watch, convinced that I had disturbed an otter at work and convinced it would return. But in the hour and a half that followed, the only creature that turned up to sample the bared flesh of the duck was a robin. It stepped quietly down through the twiggy branches and dark river shadows, perched on the carcass, and stabbed pink morsels for itself.

I returned to the scene in the dusk, but the carcass was scraps of bone. I found a few feathers impaled wetly on twigs, the bank thick with otter tracks and spraints.

I applaud those who seek to improve the lot of otters in such a place. There *should* be otters here.

The swans *should* be immune to their presence. But the second facet of the conspiracy dictated otherwise.

The cob has always laid claim to a huge territory, perhaps a square mile of water. If he is in the east bay, or on the lochan to the north, or far down the west shore of the main loch, he is out of sight of the pen sitting on her nest. That fact alone diminishes his effectiveness as a guardian. But a sitting pen is a stoic. She will starve herself for a month if necessary, and still fend off all natural threats, as long as she is in good health.

She was sitting on her first clutch when the conspiracy took its darkest turn. A third swan turned up, a new female.

There is no question in my mind now that one of the crucial reasons why the nest was robbed twice within a few weeks was that the cob's absences from the bay grew more and more protracted, and that he had begun to form a new relationship with the third swan. Now, all the learned texts tell you that swans mate for life. It has become a cliché of nature. Generation after generation, we swallow it whole. I believed it myself. Now I know that it is not true. Over the weeks that followed the arrival of the third bird, I sat with my back to the familiar dyke and watched the old bonds loosen; a pairing of swans perhaps twenty years old unravelled as simply as a reef knot.

When I walked to the shore closest to the reed bed, only the old pen would come to my call. She had always been the one to respond more eagerly when I called. She was always the first to raise her head and turn and swim towards me. She was the one who became confident enough, for all the wildness of that pair, that nest site, to stomp out of the water and take food from my hand. The cob was always more stand-offish. I cajoled him to eat from my hand only rarely. Always he would hiss his wariness. But as his absences grew I would talk to the sitting pen across twenty yards of open water and reed bed using simple words and a calm voice. To suggest there was communication between us would be outrageous, but I believe she regarded me as benevolent, which was all I ever asked of her. And there was one astounding moment in the midst of what would be the last crisis of her life.

SWAN

I found her idle and alone in the nest bay. She had already been robbed of her eggs and would be again. I called to her from the shore. She came at once and fed from my hand as I sat on an upturned sink that had been washed there three years before. Her head was at my eye-level when she stood erect and I looked into her deep-black eyes from a yard away. I spoke to her, I made the few swan noises I had learned to imitate. Occasionally she grunted back. She stepped into the water's edge, sat in the shallows and drank. Then, near enough for me to reach out and touch her (a thing I never did, nor ever tried to), she grew still where she sat. Her eyelids flickered and drooped and finally closed. Very slowly, over several minutes, her neck fell further and further back and down towards her folded wings. Her head tipped slightly forward. For ten minutes, she slept in my shadow.

I have always tried to be dispassionate, objective, in my dealings with wildlife, as matter-of-fact as nature itself. But I recognised the single emotion that was my response to the sleeping swan, and it was love, as pure as it was undeniable.

◉ ◉ ◉

If I may return my story to the season in which I began it, that autumn with stag-to-stag echoes on the air, the landscape aflame and new snow on the summits in the mountainous north. On the loch below me now there are three swans. Two are together and one is on its own. The paired birds are the new pen and the old cob. The bird on her own is his outcast mate. Several times a day he lunges down the loch at her, driving her out of what has been her own territory, pushing her further and further south. Several times a day she swims back up the loch until she crosses some unseen threshold of tolerance, and the cob lunges again, feet and wings thrashing the water, all noise and spectacle and intimidating bluster. She turns again and swims fearfully away.

All this was difficult enough for the swans. And although it is a paltry consideration by comparison, it was also difficult for the swan-watcher. I had grown so confident in my relationship with the old pairing, especially the pen, that it had become fundamental to my working life, a safe haven for my instincts, my closest contact with nature. Now it was as if that relationship had never been. None of the birds responded to my call, and even if, by carefully screening my approach down the loch, I could reach the small headland where the old pen was now accustomed to preen alone, she would swim out into the loch at the first sight or sound of me. It was as if I too was a part of the conspiracy that had robbed her of her eggs and her mate.

I did the only thing I could do. I put into practice the most basic lesson I had learned in pursuit of the secrets of nature and swans. I would go again and again, sit by the dyke and walk the shore for as long as it took. Let nature resolve its own dilemma. I would watch and question and eventually nature would answer.

It was inevitable that winter would play a decisive hand in shaping the outcome. It arrived early, the big snows falling in mid-November, after which the snowline had retreated and advanced up and down the mountains around the loch, and the floods rose with every snowmelt. The nest bay became a difficult, chancy corner.

Now, in January, winter has contrived a long, dry freeze, troubled only by the lightest snows. The wind is sharp teeth. The reed bed, which was six feet tall and vivid dark green tipped with gold in the summer and fiery in autumn, is now flat and pale fawn, a dead thing, or at least a slumberous and icebound one. It has all been too much for the outcast swan. Even now, as a thin, lazy wind brings snow drifting down out of the mountains, there are only two swans on the loch. They are the old cob and the new pen, and they are indisputably a pair.

It is a few weeks since I first noticed that the old pen was missing. I was unconcerned at first, for there are hidden bays on the loch and other watersheets nearby which the swans visit occasionally to feed for a few winter days at a time. But after two weeks of her absence it is clear that something has changed, and I have begun to search the banks. Finally, I find what I am looking for, what I feared I would find. A small mound of white feathers lies on a tussock of grass made grey by a Highland winter. It is all the monument there will ever be to the life of a swan. All around are scraps of bone and fox droppings,

[handwritten margin note: Delicate, direct prose is occasionally punctuated by metaphor.]

20

nature's last rites. As far as nature is concerned, it is all of no more account than the new snowflakes that swither down on to the feathers and disappear as they land. It begins to explain something of what has happened over these last few extraordinary seasons, and my best guess is this:

Possibly as early as last spring (perhaps even the spring before when the nest was first robbed), the old pen began to fail. The first to recognise it would have been her mate. And because all swans, even mute swans so familiar to us, are nature at heart, and concerned therefore less with the individual than the wellbeing of the tribe, the cob took advantage of the new pen's arrival. Even in the midst of the nesting season he had set about creating anew the kind of relationship that could sustain swan life on the loch.

So what the foxes found was either a bird failing and enfeebled by winter, a wounded bird (wounded by her own mate in one desperate attempt to clear her out of the territory once and for all), or even a dead bird. They dragged the carcass to this spot 300 yards from the lochside, broke it into manageable proportions and carried these off into the forest. And the swan will help the foxes and last year's cubs to get through the winter. Any rational assessment must conclude that that is fair enough, nature sustaining nature, and fate fit enough for any of nature's creatures. But I came to know that swan better than any other bird or animal I have ever encountered, and confronted by that tiny white pyre of feathers, what I feel is a kind of mourning.

But it doesn't do. All that has happened is that nature has found a way of ensuring that swan life goes on and that is what should matter to me too. In truth, the only one who feels any sense of loss is the swan-watcher, not the swan.

◉ ◉ ◉

For 20,000 years that we can be sure of, people have revered swans. In every continent except Africa and Antarctica, native people have conferred sanctity on swans and woven them into their own rituals and legends. So I am not alone, but perhaps just a little out of my own time. At the heart of many of those legends is a single idea – that the human

soul flies on in the swan after death. I know of old
people in the Western Isles of Scotland, and have
heard of others in the west of Ireland, who counsel
against harming a swan because you may harm the
human soul within, and that may be the soul of
a loved one and there is no way of knowing. It is
an understandable phenomenon. The idea of an
afterlife in a place other than on Earth is almost
universal – a Heaven, a Tir na n'Og, a Valhalla,
a Happy Hunting Ground, places of the skies. To
reach such a place, the soul must have wings, and
what better conveyance than the exquisite and
seemingly unstoppable flight of swans (there are no
pylon lines in the Dreamtime). I have rummaged
among such legends from two hemispheres and
five continents and there are more similarities than
differences. But now, standing on my own lochside,
I have a question that no human legend is equipped
to answer: who cares for the soul of a swan?

◉ ◉ ◉

It is the first tangible day of a new spring. There
is admittedly new snow on the mountains, but it is

high up and half-hearted; winter's back is broken. In the mountains, the ravens and the golden eagles are already sitting on eggs. On the loch the swan pairing has held. They swim companionably close in the sunlight. The portents are good. The death of the old pen seems to have had a liberating effect. The birds are more relaxed. The pair bond grows more sure of itself.

Several times every week I have gone down to the same shore by the nest bay and called whenever the birds have been within earshot. For weeks they ignored it. But then one day I call to them where they stand preening by the mouth of the river. I see the cob's head go up and turn. I call again. He casts off and the pen follows. I call them all the way across the bay. I make swan noises as they come close to the shore. The cob answers, four piercing falsetto grunts delivered with head and neck high and wings fanned open. They stay to feed.

I go back again and again. I call to them again and again. The response varies. It is not as it was, for it had always been the old pen that initiated the response, the cob that followed. The new pen

24

is much less confident. I am not yet a part of her landscape.

Soon they will confront the trials of a new nesting season, the floods and the otters. They will do so without the raft because I have removed it. I think I may have a provided a firmer platform than the swan's own soft and yielding structure would have been for an otter to stand on while it took the eggs. In terms of sustaining the continuity of swan life on the loch, the raft failed completely. Nature, for all the adversities it heaps on the swans, never did that.

◉ ◉ ◉

A new day, the air skittish with young spring. I called as the swans crossed the mouth of the bay a quarter of a mile out. Their necks straightened and their heads turned. They changed course through ninety degrees and swam straight in, led for the first time by the pen. She did not pause at the water's edge but moved boldly forward and fed from my hand. I moved back and sat down so that our eyes were at the same level. She came forward and the cob came with her. I had become part of her landscape.

[handwritten marginalia: How far can man ~ nature be part of the same landscape? Are our worlds distinct?]

[handwritten note at bottom: Veneration of animal world.]

25

We shared a lazy noontide hour until the clamorous flight of two whooper swans low over the nest bay jarred the cob back into awareness of his responsibilities. They landed on a small lochan to the north of the reed bed and the cob set off in a swirl of water, swimming hard. He could have flown to the lochan in seconds but he chose to swim, forging a path through the reeds into a channel of floodwater that still linked the lochan to the main loch. He had to negotiate bushes, small trees and rocks, but as soon as he burst onto the lochan his head went back, his wings went high, and he charged. The whoopers fled, calling loudly, swimming fast across the lochan; but a swimming whooper is no match for a mute swan cob with its hackles raised. He had closed to fifty yards before he flew, low and direct, and crashed on to the water between the two whoopers. They split, and flew in opposite directions, joined forces again in the air and circled across the river to land in the east bay of the main loch. The cob rose on his tail, snorted, rolled forward, throwing water over himself, then stood and opened his wings wide. Then he turned, cruised back across the lochan, through the flood channel and past his mate in the nest bay, and kept going. He swam through the bay, round the mouth of the river, round its small island, and barged into the east bay. This time he flew from 200 yards away, thrashing the water with his feet and wings for maximum effect, a choreography of nature designed to impress. The whoopers were impressed. They took off, crossed the river, and landed again on the lochan. I watched the cob. Surely not?

He landed on the water, turned and swam back, back through the east bay, round the island and the river mouth, through the nest bay, the reed bed and the flood channel, and sped into the lochan with gladiatorial panache. The whoopers flew again, this time no further than the other end of the lochan. The cob kept going, still swimming, his head sunk back on his spine, his wings hoisted mainsails. He flew from fifty yards. The whoopers flew, circled back and landed on the lochan. He turned and swam at them again, now with a tailwind that fanned his wings even higher. He pushed the whoopers before him like a collie working truculent ewes. He drove them until they could take no more, and this time they flew far down the loch.

I had run to the shore of the lochan to watch the last encounter, and I was standing by the entrance to the flood channel when he stormed past. He had made such a fuss of my presence in the nest bay an hour before, but now he gave me not so much as a glance. The pen, which had followed frantically in his wake but rarely managed to keep within 200 yards of him, caught up with him in the channel and fell in behind him. Swans this wild let you into only a certain portion of their lives. They give you intimate glimpses. But you can never have any part in the business of being a swan. You can offer them no more than the flung tribute of your admiring glance. But days like this lock me ever more willingly and inextricably into their world.

I retired uphill to the drystone dyke to consider what I had just watched, that supreme confirmation of the cob's undiminished devotion to his territory. I addressed the obvious question: why *swim* all that distance repeatedly – two half-mile diversions round the river mouth – when he could have flown across in seconds and kept the whoopers constantly on the move? The answer was a long time coming, and it is a best guess rather than a certainty. The guess is that the cob defines his territory as a piece of water. What goes on in the airspace above it is of no concern to him. Squadrons of whooper swans would not trouble him because the air poses no threat. All threats are water-borne, so they are all countered on water. Perhaps he also knows that he cannot outfly whooper swans but that they have no answer to his swimming powers. So he makes his point the only way it occurs to him to make it, by formidably cruising his territory.

◎ ◎ ◎

Spring waxes. The early morning loch is flat, milkily colourless, the sun unroused. I watch from the drystone dyke. The birds are feeding side by side, thrusting their heads below the surface, occasionally upending to reach deep. Slowly, a loose rhythm infiltrates their movements. Heads dip and rise together, a ragged togetherness at first but evolving into perfect synchronism. They turn to face each other, heads first north then south, north, south, north, south, north, south. They reach back to their tails and drag their heads forward along their flanks. Then they rise on the water breast to breast and their necks intertwine. I think there is nothing in all nature that outshines that lustrous lacing of curves, nothing in all theatre that outperforms its pivotal tension. Perhaps the first twist of the first Celtic knot was fashioned by the hands of a swan-watcher.

The necks part, the pen goes low on the water, offers her nape. The cob takes it and the moment is consummated. The pen is thrust underwater. The bay rocks. Again and again they rise on the water face-to-face, heads high, wings wide, carolling the raucous score of confirmation. Then they bathe violently. The bay rocks again. And so it begins anew.

Success will be one healthy cygnet bowing its dowdy grey-brown arch of neck to drink in the fiery waters of its first autumn – success for swan and swan-watcher. But in the year ahead I will pause often to remember the snowflakes alight on a few white feathers and disappear where they touch down, acknowledgement of the singular swan that stands apart in my life from all the company of swans.

◎ ◎ ◎

Late May, the loch grown green. The cob snaps off a reed at its base and throws it over his shoulder on to the water behind him. The heap of reeds grows, reed on reed, over hours. The pen has been feeding just beyond the reed bed. Now she swims in to help with the nest-building. It is not the first nest of spring, it is the fifth. They have already lost four nests and eighteen eggs to the floods and the otters. In the last hour it has begun to rain again, very hard. The loch starts to rise.

Nature repeats. cycles .

TWO

LOCH DOCHART IS an unsung water, a tree-shrouded blur from the A85 where the sparse human traffic of the autumn and winter months sees only an empty lay-by between Bridge of Orchy and Crianlarich with little or nothing to recommend it. The wintering whooper swans and the swan-watcher know better. It is a dark water in the narrowest part of a wide glen, an east-west trough that binds southern and central Highlands in a single glacial convulsion. Oak woods garland the north shore, golden eagles down from Rannoch ease across the northern skyline, speculating above the high slopes. Across the glen, Ben More rears all but 4,000 feet, a colossal landmark wearing the first snows of a new autumn. In this landscape of grand gestures, a white-tailed eagle folds an eight-feet wingspan as it briefly takes possession of the topmost stones of the ruinous castle on its wooded island. This particular eagle tribe is a growing presence on their coast-to-coast march between the Tay estuary and Mull, pausing on the loch to lift a trout or a goldeneye, which means one less for the neighbourhood otters. And for many years I have been inclined to drift that way myself whenever October dawns in search of the first whooper swan arrivals of autumn. Icelandic whoopers will mostly use the west coast migration routes en route for Caerlaverock on the Solway and all points south, and edge inland by way of Lorne and Loch Etive. And just as the sea eagles often encounter their kin from the opposite coast somewhere between here and Loch Tay, so Icelandic swans may eye Scandinavian swans here too, and for the same reason: it is the most obvious east-west route in the land, with big lochs and rivers all the way between the firths of Tay and Lorne. This glen is open to the west and the east and nowhere else. *The Eagle's Way** is also the whooper swan's way.

◉   ◉   ◉

**The Eagle's Way* (Saraband, 2014) explores the cross-country travels of golden and sea eagles along this route.

Autumn shades on the mountains and the trees of the north shore and the castle island, all of that landscape ablaze in just-before-sunset light. A new voice is on the cold breeze and at its first syllables an old thrill grabs the back of my throat and my heart turns over. They come round the hill from the west and the sound swells and echoes back from the rocks. They hit the sunlight and they darken to silhouettes against the western sky, but at once every movement of each wing of every bird (so twenty-two wings) shadows and sparkles as it rises and falls and the sun interweaves its own persuasive spells with the sorcery of swans.

It is not a spectacular sunset of blood orange and blackcurrant skies, but rather the pale yellow of much-too-thin custard, but it contrives a scintillating lemon shade out of whooper swans' wings. The position of the birds relative to the position of the sun in the sky, just before it begins to dip below the lowest horizon, creates further magic. For every individual bird's wingspan is lit differently from the next; and as if the effect of that were not psychedelic enough, the individual wings of every bird are also lit differently, for as the wings rise the sun illuminates the underside of the right wing and shadows its top, but simultaneously lights the top of the left wing and shadows the underside. The process reverses with every wingspan's every downstroke.

The light show has its own score (the muted brass of flugelhorns might get close to it), and no other voice in nature so authentically distils the brogue of the Arctic. "I hear it in the deep heart's core," in the words of the immortal Yeats.

These first syllables of this new autumn's first swans also put in mind a verse in a poem by my dear departed friend, Marion Campbell, and which I read at her funeral. The poem is called *Levavi Oculos*, which means something like "I have lifted my eyes", and it appeared in her timeless and exquisitely written book, *Argyll, the Enduring Heartland* (Turnstone Books, 1977). This is the verse that suddenly sings in my head:

And hark! What others come?
Wild swans, the soul of storm,

ENCOUNTERS IN THE WILD

Beating their great vans in the sky
And from long golden throats
Sounding out haunting notes,
The trumpets of an older chivalry;
And tilting in the wind, the eagles
Not of Rome.

Sometimes nature contrives rather more sensation than I can comfortably handle at one time. The eleven swans advance down the glen towards the loch where I sit on a shoreline rock, and as they start to glide down towards its now black surface they lose the sunlight and are suddenly and simply pure swan. But just as suddenly, the clamour of their voices magnifies as though a volume control has been manipulated. I have been so absorbed in their arrival from the west that I fail to register a skein of thirty more homing in on the loch from the east. I realise what is happening only moments before these new swans touch down at the east end of the loch, and cruise on their own reflections towards the west and a frantic, raucous, celebratory greeting with the others. Whooper swans are

the most sociable of creatures, and any meeting
with other groups or solitary travellers of their
own kind involves a group hug of open wings, tall
necks, and the brassiest ensemble you ever heard in
a Highland landscape. Loch Dochart has a particularly potent echo if you sit in the right place, and
right here, right now, I find myself at the still centre
of a whirlpool of coruscating spectacle and sound.
Not for the first time in my writing life, I find myself
spellbound by swans.

The book that propelled me towards this particular life with a forceful thud in the small of my back
was Gavin Maxwell's *Ring of Bright Water* (Longman,
1960), such was its impact on my eighteen-year-old
self. I was astounded by the writing, and in particular by his affecting reunion with his otter Mij after
it had gone AWOL all night and all the following
day. Maxwell unashamedly declared that Mij meant
more to him than most human beings, and that he
would miss the otter more than any of them: "I
knew that Mij trusted me more utterly than did any
of my own kind, and so supplied a need that we are
slow to admit."

With the huge caveat that the human relationships in my own life are infinitely more stable than his ever were, there have been times – exclusively in the company of swans – when I have felt illuminating shafts of compassion and understanding of his startling declaration.

Even as the whooper swans and their tumult and the crumpled waters of Loch Dochart begin to calm down and a restless species of order begins to emerge and the diminuendo of the ensemble begins to splinter into short phrases of solo voices then finally into querulous monosyllables, I am already archiving the hour and its landscape setting, already weighing its preciousness to me, already folding its events into a personal treasury of the immortal hours of nature that I have witnessed first hand, knowing it would prove to be among the most durable of all.

I returned to the loch two days later and there was not a swan in sight. Sometimes it is all a matter of simply being in the right place at the right time. But it is also true that the more often you go, the luckier you are likely to be.

THREE

Skye in midwinter, dwindling down to the darkest, briefest day and longest night, is at its most approachable. The tourist trade doesn't trouble it and neither do the midges, and both of these can torment a nature-writer's spirit if he finds he has washed up here in high summer through circumstances beyond his control.

Loch Suardal lies in the west of the island, a mile or two north beyond Dunvegan. It is as unprepossessing a watersheet as any you ever laid eyes on, but whenever I lay my eyes on it or think about it from afar, I see a pearl, satin-sheened by a midday twilight the day before the winter solstice, and smirr-softened.

The Suardal Burn drags a dozen skinny tributaries down from the blunt, peaty flanks of Beinn

Bhreac, a lumpy hill that thickens the headland between Loch Dunvegan and Loch Bay of
Waternish. No one ever wrote a poem or a song
about Loch Suardal or Beinn Bhreac. Skye's many
glories lie elsewhere.

The Suardal Burn nudges into the north-west
corner of the loch, which is small, shallow, peaty
and reedy. The burn's left bank projects beyond the
loch shore as a slim peninsula fifty yards long, so
that there is the flowing water of the burn to one
side, the still water of the loch to the other. That
spit of land is a yard high, a couple of yards wide
and flat-topped. I found it drifted by the snow birds.
Twenty whooper swans were strung out along its
length and in the shallows just beyond it, dozing
fitfully through one more drab winter day.

A single-track road to nowhere-very-much
wrapped itself round the west side of the loch,
climbing gently as it unravelled, so that it was fully
fifty feet above the swans at its nearest point to their
roost. I have the kind of car (small, light, four-wheel-
drive, good ground clearance) that skips eagerly
offroad into tiny spaces that offer good vantage

points. It duly skipped into one such space and I lowered the window, switched off the engine, and felt at once the island quiet almost as a physical force.

Nature contrives few more ideal roosts for wild swans than this. It is sheltered from Loch Dunvegan and all its ocean winds by a low ridge; it is favoured with good feeding, which for a swan means plentiful submerged pondweed; and it is just large enough to accommodate twenty whooper swans should they all decide to take off at once. I settled to await the impact of my discreet arrival on the swans, but no swan stirred. Only one head out of twenty was raised, and while it was certainly watching me it was quite unmoved, quite unalarmed. If they had been there for any length of time they would know that the road's sparse winter traffic is only a problem if it decants a mammal after it comes to a stop.

I produced a flask and a sandwich, poured coffee and watched the swans. This is what I mean when I use the expression "a working lunch". So I watched for a while, trying to imprint on my mind certain attitudes and shapes among the folded swans; I made a few sketchy notes and a few un-noteworthy sketches, but mostly I just watched, for I am rarely happier in the company of nature than when that company takes the form of whooper swans either in flight (surely among the most beautiful natural events on earth) or like this, relaxed and content and at close quarters in a wild and familiar landscape.

It bears repeating from time to time: nature is at its most revealing when you keep still and quiet and let it come to you. I had been there about an hour (during which all that had happened was the occasional rearrangement of the folds of a particular folded swan) when I was startled by the cry of a solitary widgeon I had not seen. It was an anxious, piercing cry like the second half of a strenuously delivered wolf-whistle. Moments later the bird appeared swimming fast downstream. As soon as it reached open water it launched itself almost vertically into the air.

Cue instant mayhem. Salvoes of widgeon, mallard and goldeneye exploded out of the reeds and out of silence into raucous, spring-heeled flight that rocked the airspace above the loch. My hasty guess was 150 birds. I was about to follow them in the binoculars when a heron burst in on the chaos, apparently in hot pursuit of the solitary widgeon. It came fast downriver, screaming. And more or less as the swimming widgeon became airborne and panicked the reed bed hordes, the heron must have seen the swans.

Now every swan neck was unfolded and every swan head periscope-high, a straight line of twenty raised necks and swivelling heads. The heron changed tack, having lost the widgeon. It swerved left and lunged at the first swan head, causing it to duck in self-defence. Then, like one of those arrangements of dominoes you can topple by touching the first one, it flew right down the line at swan-head height, causing each head to duck in turn. But unlike the domino trick, as the heron passed over, each collapsed neck straightened again and each head uttered an astonished "Woop?"

The heron rasped three more shrieks in the course of its domino run, then twice more for the benefit of a tight little raft of ducks that still sat on the water. Then it crossed the ridge towards Loch Dunvegan and vanished. The ducks that had flown circled several times then drifted down sporadically back onto the surface of Loch Suardal. The swans responded with a bout of vigorous preening, cracking their open wings like wet sails in a gale.

I was still trying to make sense of it all when a new movement caught my eye just above the spruce wood on the far shore. A sea eagle was taking off from the gloomy green depths of the treetops with that now-familiar-to-me collapsing parachute routine of its first few wingbeats. I stirred its presence into the mix and concocted a theory, which goes like this:

The heron had been fishing somewhere upstream and out of sight, and the sea eagle had drifted by and taken a speculative pass at it. As the sea eagle grows ever more confident of its place in the island West (a land-and-sea-scape well littered with herons), such attacks are not at all unusual. The heron, startled, annoyed, fearful, but unscathed, flew low and downstream, and as the eagle pulled out, the hapless solitary widgeon was in the heron's path. The heron screamed, the widgeon swam fast downstream, then detected something abnormally malevolent in the heron and flew, too fast and too agile for its pursuer.

Then the heron saw the swans sitting up, a row of heads arranged like a coconut shy, and vented its discomfort by shying at every coconut. By the time the heron had vanished, the eagle had disappeared into the gloom. The ducks had landed again and settled down. And I had turned my attention back to the swans, which was after all why I had stopped here in the first place. Slowly, in ones and twos, they resumed their folded demeanour, all but one, which kept a fitful lookout over sky, dark wood, and the ridge behind the car.

"Write," said Margiad Evans in *Autobiography* (Arthur Baker, 1943), "from your eyes and ears, and your touch, in the very now where you find yourself alive wherever it may be… Conceal yourself in the fields. Watch and be in what you see or in what you feel in your brain. There is no substitute even in divine imagination for the touch of the moment, the touch of the daylight on the dream."

It is the best piece of advice for a nature writer that I have ever encountered, I swallowed it whole and I put it into practice constantly, and pass it on whenever I can.

And on a murky twilit midday on Skye, the setting of so many of my living dreams, and in the company of the dream birds, the wild whooper swans, I sat on and wrote in the very now where I found myself, the writing illuminated by the touch of the moment, the touch of the daylight on the dream, as the afternoon dwindled down and darkened towards the end of the last daylight before the winter solstice.

FOUR

I HAVE RETURNED to the Perthshire loch that began
it all. The view opens out just as the public road
ends and gives way to a forestry track. At this point
the reed bed is still half a mile away but I put the
glasses on it anyway. It is at its most conspicuous
in early spring, for it is the only thing in that landscape of loch and forest and mountainside that is
the colour of cold milky tea.

What I am looking for is a splash of white in the
sunshine. One of the great advantages of watching
swans is that you can spot them from a great
distance. But today there is no splash of white in
sight. I resettle the small pack on my shoulders and
head off along the track. And so it begins again,
this ritual of more than thirty springs now, this walk
along the so-familiar track through an intimate
landscape.

There have been hundreds of return journeys by now. Memories crowd round. Two books grew out of this routine, a series of radio programmes, a television programme, a clutch of poems, and I shudder to think how many newspaper and magazine articles. And still I cannot stay away from the place and its centre-stage swans. I gave up years ago trying to explain to myself my fascination with the tribe of wild swans, but as the years pass it only deepens and the birds constantly reward my persistence with small surprises, confided secrets, and one miracle.

The winter before the one that has just ended was long and hard, and the five-miles-long loch froze from end to end. I had never seen that before in the thirty-something years I have known it, and locals with much longer memories could not remember it either. It was unprecedented, they said, and the temperature fell and fell until it reached −20°C and stayed there for several nights; it may have been unprecedented but this winter it happened again. Swans can handle cold but it can be hard on first-year birds. So, about the miracle…

SWAN

Two Aprils ago the current pair's nest site in the reed bed suffered the all-too-familiar fate – nine springs out of ten the river floods, and if the hills have been holding deep snow, the floods are spectacular. Nine springs out of ten, the swans lose their first nest and their first clutch of eggs; and their second nest and their second clutch of eggs; and their third… and the worst I have known was a year they lost five nests and twenty-nine eggs before they finally gave up.

So two years ago they lost four nests and in July they gave up. They began travelling far down the loch beyond the nest territory, and even flew four miles up the glen to a small pond where they gorged themselves for a week on its luxuriant pondweed. By mid-July the reed bed is seven or eight feet tall, the reeds a deep dark green tipped with gold, a majestic place in a sunny summer wind when it rustles and gleams as it dances.

By mid-July too, I had relaxed my swan routines in the face of another failed season and was spending the good days high in the hills watching golden eagles, and whatever else came my way. I was also

49

travelling and researching a book about wolves, so I had a lot on my plate. By mid-August I was spending too much time at the writing desk for my liking and when one rainy day brightened into a beautiful late afternoon and early evening I wandered down the track to the loch with no expectations other than the pleasure of the walk and the taste of the air.

I reached the reed bed just in time to see the mute swan cob respond to my slow advance along the shore by dodging out of sight into the reeds. Strange, I thought, so I did what I always do when I see something strange in nature, I sat down and waited to see if the strangeness explained itself. But two hours later, no swan had appeared and I walked home, wondering.

And early next morning I was still wondering when I walked back along the track. I took a more considered approach towards the reed bed, passing through a boggy little wood of alder and birch scrub and with as much discretion as I could muster. From the screen of the trees I could see the two adult swans in the bay, a few yards beyond the outer edge of the reed bed. They were no more than fifty yards away, but they were close together and demonstrably nervous, and at that moment I dared to wonder if they had cygnets nearby, if they had reared a brood in the unlikeliest of circumstances, and so I watched them in the glasses and scoured every inch of the bay and the reed bed edges in search of the unthinkable. Nothing.

But then I heard the sound of the unthinkable.

The voice of a very young cygnet is the thinnest, briefest, highest-pitched semi-quaver you can imagine, a bit like the contact call of a dunnock, but repeated over and over again, or like the sound of a creaking wheelbarrow wheel in the distance. I listened hard (I could still see nothing) and it seemed to me there was only one voice. Maybe it *was* a creaking wheelbarrow in the distance?

Then the tiny grey head and black eye and stubby black beak of a single cygnet appeared in the middle of its mother's back, and I was watching the unthinkable. Under the dense green midsummer reed bed's cloak the swans had hatched a secret cygnet.

Those naturalists and field-guide compilers who deal in statistical averages and expect nature to conform to them will tell you that with swans, the earlier the hatch, the better the bird's chances of survival, and that one this late was doomed to an early death. But this was a young pair of adults in only their third nesting season, and they had already shown the extraordinary perseverance and energy demanded of five attempts at nesting in four months. Not only that, my long experience of this nest site has taught me that the demands of its exposed Highland situation and its often freakish weather have so conditioned all its resident swans that what the field guides would consider to be extraordinary behaviour has become the norm.

The cygnet was tumbled into the world at a time of plenty. Summer lingered and gave way to a long, beautiful and benevolent autumn. The parents had only one cygnet to attend to and attend to it they did. Mute swans are notoriously offhand parents. These were the most diligent I have ever seen.

When winter finally kicked in at New Year, it was particularly severe and so the loch had frozen over for the first time. The cygnet still looked improbably small and brown to be capable of withstanding such a winter, but it looked fit and well-fed. The parents stuck close right through the winter and it was late March before they responded to the new nesting season by ousting their secret cygnet from the territory. I was walking down the forest track that March one late afternoon when I heard the familiar wing-rhythm of a mute swan in flight – there was a brownish-white bird flying low above the trees that fringe the river. It was the first time I had seen it in the air, and I stood still and waved and I watched it go until it was too small to watch, and I wished it bon voyage.

◉ ◉ ◉

So the reed bed is still half a mile away when I stop to put the binoculars on it, then resettle my pack on my shoulders and head off along the track. Five miles away at the south end of the loch, a single swan had turned up in the autumn and lingered right through the winter. It's still there. Its pale beak shows that it is a juvenile bird, not yet old enough to breed. I have no way of knowing of course, but I can't help wondering.

FIVE

The poetry of earth is never dead
John Keats

THE POETRY OF EARTH
A swan is a sonnet, she knows
fourteen ways to rhyme, she nests
by seven willows – these cast
about her a net of seven shadows

that whisper ancient fears,
told and retold since glaciers held sway
then warming slunk away.

And earth is a couplet – land and sea,
you and me, swan and willow tree.

AFTERWORD

THE MUTE SWAN (*Cygnus olor*) is the one everybody knows, resident of parkland ponds, canals, tranquil rivers, ornamental lakes in stately homes, but as demonstrated in this book, also of some remarkably wild places. And it is far from mute. It has a wide and unflattering vocabulary of grunts, snorts, hisses and cheeps (the speciality of cygnets from newly hatched to fully-fledged, at which point they sound ridiculous). There is also a far-carrying wing-song in flight that has the power to put a lump in the throat of a fully-fledged nature writer, and which is unique to mute swans. One scientific theory is that it acts as a contact call between birds flying at night or in poor visibility because it utters no sound in flight, whereas all other swans are vocal in flight. Another theory is that the word "mute" is derived from a much older and obscure word meaning "sounder", and which relates specifically to the sound of the wings.

The origins of the terms "cob" and "pen" to denote male and female are lost in antiquity. The terms are at least as old as England's bizarre Swan Laws, first published as The Act for Swans in 1482, and formalised during the reign of Edward VII (1547–53) and revised in 1563. The concept of the mute swan as a "royal bird" is much older. There is evidence as early 966 in the reign of King Edgar, and the concept of crown ownership of all the swans in England was already well established by then. Over the centuries, English monarchs dispensed gifts of local ownership of swans to sundry nobles, and the historic principle, in gesture form at least, still survives by way of the outrageous anachronism of swan-upping on the River Thames, where the birds are rounded up and "marked" every year. Perhaps in time, the more modern-looking royal generation waiting in the wings will put an end to it once and for all and give mute swans back to nature.

SWAN

The whooper swan (*Cygnus cygnus*) is the furthest-flung of all the swans, with a natural distribution from Iceland in the west to Japan in the east. It is almost exclusively an autumn and winter visitor to Britain and from two distinct populations: the great majority are from Iceland and the rest from Scandinavia. Their time on these shores is a restless one and they are almost constantly on the move between regular gathering sites from the Northern Isles to the Ouse Washes in Norfolk and mid-Wales. But most birds winter in Scotland, with large flocks at Caerlaverock on the Solway, Loch Leven on the Kinross-Fife border, the Insh Marshes in Strathspey, the Loch of Strathbeg and Loch Eye on the north-east coast, and the Uists in the Western Isles. There are hopeful signs that the small breeding population in the Northern Isles and the West Highlands is increasing, a piecemeal return to the landscape from which it was once exterminated.

The goose-sized Bewick's swan (*Cygnus columbianus*) is a regular winter visitor in Scotland, albeit in sparse numbers, and mostly at Caerlaverock and Loch Leven. As if its momentous migration from

Siberia was not long enough, it mostly bypasses Scotland for its main gathering places at the Ouse and Nene Washes and Slimbridge.

The only other swan you might see in Britain is the Australian black swan (*Cygnus atratus*), a favourite in wildfowl collections and the gardens of stately homes, from which a few have inevitably escaped. One pair I know nests on a canal at Ratho near Edinburgh. Individual birds often keep the company of other swans in winter, where they look like nothing so much as a negative of a swan.

Few of nature's creatures are quite so liberally and chaotically entwined in human mythology as swans, from Greek and Scandinavian gods (Zeus and Apollo were at the centre of the mythological industry that ensnared Michelangelo and Yeats among many, many others), to Shakespeare, who bought the whole "swan song" nonsense – but being Shakespeare he used it to potent effect and the phrase has passed into the language as shorthand for a final fling, a last bow. Swans do not sing, either in life or in their death throes. I have heard biologists discuss the theory that whooper swans in particular, being possessed of a particularly long windpipe, can produce a prolonged final exhalation that emerges as an audible sound. I don't know. I have never had a swan die on me. I have met quite a few vets and SSPCA staff and swan hospital staff, all of whom have had many swans die on them, and none of these has heard a dying swan sing.

Other urban myths cling to swans too. The paired-for-life thing I have dealt with already, and just like people, some of them do and some of them don't. The other commonplace entry in the book of swan-nonsense is that a swan can break your arm. I have heard this spouted so often by people who should know better and by people who don't know one end of a swan from the other. The truth is that if a swan does actually break your arm it will be because (a) you have done something ridiculously stupid to a swan, (b) you have then been astonishingly unlucky, and (c) you are remarkably brittle-boned.

In combat with other swans, or occasionally with tormenting dogs, a swan will use the "elbows" of its wings like clubs. Very, very occasionally two cobs will fight to the death, but almost invariably the weaker one will opt for retreat long before serious injury is accomplished.

◉ ◉ ◉

Organisations with a special interest in swan conservation include the Wildfowl and Wetland Trust and the Swannery at Abbotsbury in Dorset.

www.wwt.org.uk

www.abbotsbury-tourism.co.uk/swannery

AUTHOR'S NOTE

THE FIRST PART OF this book originally appeared as a very slim volume called *The Company of Swans* (The Harvill Press, 1997), illustrated with engravings by Harry Brockway. It has been out of print for some years but I have had more inquiries about it than anything else I have ever written.

When Sara Hunt at Saraband first suggested the *Encounters in the Wild* series we agreed that it presented the perfect opportunity to bring the story of *The Company of Swans* back to life. I'm very grateful to Sara for that opportunity, because it is a piece of work for which I have a particular affection. I hope you agree that it merits a second chance. I have altered the original text only in a few slight details, and only in the interests of grammar and accuracy and the removal of the odd jarring phrase that must have seemed felicitous at the time. It remains essentially the story of a pair of remarkable swans, both of which lived well over twenty years. They are obviously long dead now, and other swans have taken their place and tried to come terms with the same recurring pattern of natural events. But none has shown the same qualities of persistence, courage and raw wildness as the two birds whose story is told here, birds I only ever knew as the old cob and the old pen, the latter a bird that rather got under my skin in a way that no wild creature has done before or since.

JIM CRUMLEY IS A NATURE WRITER, journalist, poet, and passionate advocate for our wildlife and wild places. He is the author of thirty books, and is a newspaper and magazine columnist and an occasional broadcaster on both BBC radio and television.

He has written companions to this volume on the barn owl, fox and hare, and there are further ENCOUNTERS IN THE WILD titles planned. He has also written in depth on topics as diverse as beavers, eagles, wolves, whales, native woods, mountains and species reintroductions.

Published by Saraband
Suite 202, 98 Woodlands Road
Glasgow, G3 6HB
www.saraband.net

Copyright © Jim Crumley 2015

All rights reserved. No part of this publication may be
reproduced, stored in a retrieval system, or transmitted,
in any form or by any means, electronic, mechanical,
photocopying, recording, or otherwise, without first
obtaining the written permission of the copyright owner.

ISBN: 9781910192122

Printed in the EU on sustainably sourced paper.
Cover illustration: Carry Akroyd